Therian Tales: Embracing Our Inner Nature

A Complete Guide to Therianthropy

By Uranzaya Batsaikhan

Copyright © 2023 Uranzaya Batsaikhan

All rights reserved

No part of this book may be reproduced, or stored in a retrieval system, or transmitted in any form or by any means, electronic, mechanical, photocopying, recording, or otherwise, without express written permission of the publisher.

Cover design by: Uranzaya Batsaikhan

To my dearest Anu,

In your gentle exploration of Therianthropy, consider this book a companion, a beacon to illuminate your understanding. It's not a path chosen, but a path that whispers to your inner soul. Through these pages, encounter the stories of others who have felt similar whispers and journeyed to understand them, discovering a realm of support and shared experiences. As you navigate these paths, remember you walk not alone. Love and understanding accompany you in each step.

With all my love, Uranzaya

CONTENT

Introduction..6
    What is a Therian?...6
    What is Therianthropy?..6
    The Importance of Understanding and Embracing Our Inner Nature.........6
    The Aim of The Book..7

Chapter 1: What is Therianthropy?..8
    Definition and Historical Context...10
    The Therianthropy Symbol: The (Theta-Delta)...10
    Different Types of Therian Experiences...11

Chapter 2: The Therian Journey..18
    Personal Anecdotes and Stories of Discovering One's Therian Identity.......20
    The Importance of Self-Discovery and Acceptance...................................22

Chapter 3: Therian Terminology and Concepts..25
    Important Terms..27
    Clarification of Common Misconceptions...31
    The Difference Between Therianthropy and Other Related Concepts........31

Chapter 4: The Role of Community..32
    Importance of Having a Support Network...34
    Online Forums and Communities..36
    Therian Gatherings and Howls..38

Chapter 5: Everyday Life as a Therian..39
    Challenges and Benefits..41
    Stories of Living a Balanced Life..43
    How to Incorporate Therian Traits into Everyday Living.........................45

Chapter 6: Navigating Relationships..49
    Romantic Relationships...51
    Friendships...53
    Family Dynamics...56

Chapter 7: Common Misunderstandings and Criticisms.....................................59
    Addressing the Skepticism Around Therianthropy....................................61
    Responding to Common Criticisms...61
    Strategies for Constructive Conversations..62

Chapter 8: The Therian Code of Ethics...63
    Respect for Nature and Animals..65
    Community Guidelines and Principles..65
    Personal Responsibility...66

Chapter 9: The Practice of Quadrobics... **67**
    The Origin of Quadrobics.. 69
    Psychological and Spiritual Benefits... 69
    Guidelines for Practicing Quadrobics Safely.. 69
Chapter 10: Modern Perspectives: A Journey Through the Digital Age and Beyond.... 70
    Online Communities.. 72
    Virtual Reality.. 72
    Skepticism and Misunderstanding... 73
Chapter 11: Embracing Your Inner Nature..**74**
    The Importance of Self-Acceptance.. 76
    Tips for Embracing Your Therian Identity.. 76
    The Role of Creativity and Imagination.. 77
Chapter 12: Your Personal Therian Experience: A Space for Reflection.............**78**
    Prompts to Consider:... 80
    A page for personal reflection... 81
    Bonus Quiz: How Therian Are You?.. 82
Conclusion..**84**
    Summary of Key Takeaways... 86
    Encouragement to Continue the Journey of Self-Discovery and Acceptance...86
Appendix...**87**
    Frequently Asked Questions.. 87
    Resource List: Books, Articles, Websites, and Communities........................... 87
Acknowledgments..**88**

Introduction

Welcome to "Therian Tales: Embracing Our Inner Nature," a journey into the fascinating, complex, and often misunderstood world of Therianthropy. This book is written for those who identify as Therians, those who are curious about the subject, and for the family and friends who seek to understand their loved ones better. Whether you've just discovered the term 'Therian' or have been a part of this community for years, this book aims to shed light on what it means to embrace one's inner nature.

What is a Therian?

A Therian is someone who internally identifies as partially or wholly non-human. This identification is a personal, spiritual connection with a specific animal, beyond physical form. Therians may experience "shifts," feeling more aligned with their animal identity, though there is no physical transformation. This self-identification deeply influences their self-perception and worldview.

What is Therianthropy?

At its core, Therianthropy is the experience of having a deep, intrinsic connection to an animal or animals, often to the point of identifying as non-human on some level. While this may sound peculiar or even unbelievable to some, it's a reality that many live with every day. Therians come from all walks of life, from various cultures and age groups, and their experiences are as diverse as they are.

The Importance of Understanding and Embracing Our Inner Nature

In a world that often pushes us toward conformity, the journey to understand and accept one's inner nature is a courageous act. For Therians, this journey is not just metaphorical but deeply personal, sometimes spiritual, and can be life-transforming.

Understanding oneself can open doors to a deeper sense of well-being, stronger relationships, and a more authentic life. Furthermore, by diving deep into the Therian experience, we also explore broader themes of identity, community, and the human-animal connection.

The Aim of The Book

This book has three primary goals:

1. **To Explore:** We will delve into the history, terminology, and various facets of Therianthropy, aiming to provide a thorough understanding of what it entails.

2. **To Explain:** Through personal stories, academic perspectives, and interviews, this book seeks to explain the complexities and nuances that come with identifying as a Therian.

3. **To Celebrate:** Above all, this book aims to celebrate the richness and diversity of the Therian community, highlighting the positive aspects and the sense of wonder that can come from embracing one's inner nature.

So, let's embark on this journey together—a journey that will take us through the forests of terminology, the oceans of personal experiences, and the skies of spiritual beliefs, all to reach a better understanding of what it means to be a Therian in today's world.

Welcome aboard!

Chapter 1: What is Therianthropy?

∞ ∞ ∞

"The mirror reflects not just a face, but the echo of a distant wild call, resounding in the depths of the soul."

∞ ∞ ∞

The term 'Therianthropy' may be unfamiliar to some, or shrouded in mystery and misconception for others. However, to those who identify as Therians, the term offers a lens through which they view and experience their world in a unique way.

This chapter aims to demystify Therianthropy by offering a comprehensive definition, exploring its historical context, identifying different types of Therian experiences, and presenting modern perspectives that have emerged, especially with the advent of online communities.

Definition and Historical Context

Definition

Therianthropy is the condition or belief where a person identifies as a non-human animal, either spiritually, psychologically, or in some other significant way. Therians do not claim to be physically non-human but feel an intrinsic, deeply rooted connection to their animal 'theriotype.'

Historical Context

The concept of humans possessing animalistic traits or transforming into animals is ancient and pervasive across various cultures. From Native American totems to shapeshifters in folklore, the idea of a deep, mystical bond between humans and animals exists in many societies. While the modern term 'Therianthropy' is relatively new, the essence of this experience is age-old.

The Therianthropy Symbol: The ⌬ (Theta-Delta)

The symbol commonly associated with the Therian community is the Θ (Theta-Delta) symbol. It consists of an uppercase Greek Theta (Θ) superimposed over a Delta (Δ). The Theta-Delta is more than just an emblem; it's a powerful representation of the community's core beliefs and experiences.

While the Theta-Delta symbol may not have ancient origins, it has quickly become a unifying symbol for Therians around the world. It gained prominence largely through online communities and has been adopted as an emblem to identify and express Therianthropy.

Symbolic Interpretations

- Theta (Θ): This is often considered to represent the spiritual or psychological aspects of being a Therian. It is the theoretical or philosophical component that many Therians explore to understand their identities.
- Delta (Δ): This signifies change or difference, a nod to the transformative experiences and shifts that are part of a Therian's life.

As with any community symbol, it's important to use the Theta-Delta respectfully. It shouldn't be used to misrepresent or stereotype the Therian community. Those who are not part of the community should be cautious and respectful in how they interact with or use the symbol.

The Theta-Delta symbol serves as a powerful visual representation of the Therian community, encapsulating its complex blend of spirituality, psychology, and transformative change. As with any symbol, its power lies not just in its design, but in the meanings and experiences it encapsulates for those who identify with it.

Different Types of Therian Experiences

1. Psychological Therianthropy

Some Therians understand their experience through the lens of psychology. They may view their Therian identity as an integral part of their psyche, developed through life experiences, personality traits, or even as a coping mechanism. Here's an exploration of this concept:

Psychological Therianthropy posits that identifying as a non-human animal is a mental phenomenon. For psychological Therians, their theriotype is viewed as a component of their psyche that influences behavior, emotions, and perceptions, but without the spiritual dimensions that some other Therians describe.

From a psychological viewpoint, Therianthropy may stem from a variety of cognitive processes:
- Subconscious Archetypes: Carl Jung's theory of archetypes suggests that primal symbols are embedded in the collective unconscious. Therians might identify with animals that embody certain archetypical traits they also see in themselves.
- Personal Identification: Therians may find aspects of their personality, behavior, or emotional responses reflected in their theriotype. This identification offers a framework for understanding oneself.

Psychological Benefits
- Self-Understanding: Many Therians report that recognizing their theriotype helps them understand their behavioral traits and emotional responses better.
- Mental Well-Being: Some Therians describe experiencing a sense of wholeness or integration after accepting their theriotype, which positively affects their mental health.

The Role of "Shifting"

In psychological Therianthropy, "shifting" refers to a change in mindset or emotional state that aligns more closely with the individual's theriotype. Unlike spiritual Therians, who may view shifts as spiritual experiences or transformations, psychological Therians often view them as mental states where the traits of their theriotype become more prominent.

- Mental Shifts: Periods where one mentally feels more like their theriotype than their human self.
- Phantom Shifts: Sensations of having non-human body parts, like a tail or wings, which are perceived mentally but not considered spiritual manifestations.

Coping and Adaptation

Understanding one's Therian nature from a psychological perspective often involves various coping mechanisms:
- Mindfulness Techniques: Some Therians use mindfulness to understand their shifts better and to integrate these experiences into their daily life.
- Channeling Traits: Utilizing aspects of their theriotype in day-to-day activities, such as using the "pack mentality" of a wolf theriotype in team settings.

Psychological Therianthropy offers a secular, mental health-focused perspective on what is often considered a spiritual or metaphysical experience. By examining the psychological components of Therianthropy, one gains valuable insights into the self, enriching both mental well-being and self-understanding.

Example 1:
Sarah: The Introverted Wolf

Sarah has always felt an intense connection with wolves. She doesn't believe in spiritual or mystical explanations but feels that her personality traits align closely with those of a wolf. For Sarah, moments of solitude aren't lonely; they're necessary for her mental health, similar to how a lone wolf needs time away from the pack.

Mental Shifts: During stressful days at work, Sarah takes brief moments to close her eyes and envision the forest, imagining she is a wolf roaming freely. These mental shifts help her manage stress.

Coping Mechanisms: Sarah has a playlist of nature sounds featuring wolves howling. She plays this in the background when she needs to focus or feel grounded.

2. Spiritual Therianthropy

For those who view Therianthropy from a spiritual perspective, the identification with a non-human animal is much more than a psychological phenomenon; it's a profound spiritual connection. This may be conceptualized as a soul bond, a past life experience, or a mystical calling.

Spiritual Therianthropy has various theoretical origins:
- Reincarnation and Past Lives: Some spiritual Therians believe that they were their theriotype in a past life, and this past life has carried over into their current human existence.

- Spirit Animals and Totems: Other Therians may see their theriotype as their spirit animal or totem, guiding them in this life, akin to some Indigenous and shamanistic beliefs.
- Soul Dualism: In this perspective, a Therian has both a human and a non-human soul cohabitating in the same body.

Spiritual Practices and Rituals

- Meditation and Journeying: Many Therians practice meditation techniques aimed at connecting deeper with their theriotype, sometimes described as "soul journeying."
- Rituals and Symbols: Some use rituals, talismans, or symbols, such as the Theta-Delta, to strengthen their connection to their theriotype.

The Role of "Shifting" in Spiritual Therianthropy

- Astral Shifting: Unlike the mental or phantom shifts described in psychological Therianthropy, spiritual Therians may describe experiences of "astral shifting," where they believe their spiritual form takes on the shape of their theriotype in an astral plane.
- Dream Shifting: Some Therians experience vivid dreams where they are their theriotype. These are often considered deeply spiritual experiences that offer guidance or messages.

Ethical and Spiritual Lessons

- Animal Wisdom: Spiritual Therians often seek to understand the innate wisdom of their theriotype, integrating these lessons into their human lives.
- Respect for Nature: A deep spiritual respect for all life forms, especially for the species one identifies with, is often a cornerstone of spiritual Therianthropy.

Challenges and Criticisms

- Cultural Appropriation: Care must be taken to respect the spiritual practices of Indigenous and other cultures that have long-standing traditions involving spirit animals or totems.
- Skepticism: As with many spiritual practices, Therians often face skepticism and must find ways to balance their spiritual beliefs with the secular world.

Spiritual Therianthropy offers a rich, multi-layered approach to understanding one's non-human identity. It provides avenues for spiritual growth, ethical living, and a profound respect for the interconnectedness of all life.

Example 2:
David: The Eagle Who Soars

David feels a spiritual connection with eagles. He believes that in a past life, he was an eagle and that his love for heights and freedom comes from this past existence.

Astral Shifting: Through meditation, David practices what he calls "astral shifting," where he feels his spirit soar above mountains and rivers as an eagle. These sessions leave him feeling rejuvenated.

Dream Shifting: David frequently dreams of flying high above landscapes, viewing the world from an eagle's perspective. He takes these dreams as spiritual signs or messages, often turning to them for guidance in making important life decisions.

Spiritual Practices: David has a small altar at home featuring feathers, a nest-like arrangement of twigs, and an eagle figurine. He spends a few minutes each morning and evening at this altar, connecting with his eagle spirit.

3. Cladotherianthropy

Cladotherianthropy challenges the norm even within the diverse world of Therianthropy. Instead of identifying with a specific animal, such as a wolf or an eagle, Cladotherians resonate with a broader category, like canines or birds of prey.

The identification as a broader category of animal can come from various sources:
- **Ambiguity in Spiritual or Psychological Experience:** Some Cladotherians don't have a specific animal they connect with, but rather a range of characteristics common to a group of animals.
- **Broad Spectrum Shifts:** Unlike regular shifts that focus on one particular animal, Cladotherians may experience a range of shifts that align with various animals within a chosen category.

Types of Cladotherianthropy
- **Genus-based:** For example, identifying with the Felis genus rather than specifying domestic cats or wildcats.
- **Family-based:** For instance, identifying with all raptors rather than just hawks or eagles.
- **Class-based:** Such as identifying with all mammals or all reptiles.

Shifting in Cladotherianthropy
- **Composite Shifts:** Some Cladotherians describe their shifts as a composite of various animals within the group they identify with. For example, a person identifying with the feline family might experience shifts that have traits of both a lion and a domestic cat.
- **Fluid Shifts:** Other Cladotherians experience fluid shifts that transition between different animals within the category they identify with.

Challenges and Complexities

- **Lack of Specificity:** One of the challenges for Cladotherians is the lack of a specific animal to research or connect with. This can sometimes make their experiences feel less anchored compared to Therians who identify with a specific species.
- **Community Understanding:** Even within the Therian community, Cladotherianthropy is not always well-understood, which can lead to feelings of isolation or marginalization.

Cladotherianthropy expands the boundaries of how we understand Therianthropy, offering an even wider scope for identifying with the animal kingdom. Whether genus-based, family-based, or class-based, Cladotherianthropy brings its own set of unique experiences, challenges, and insights, further enriching the diverse tapestry of the Therian community.

Example 3:
Emily: The Cladotherian of the Ocean

Emily has always felt a deep connection with the ocean and its inhabitants. She doesn't identify with a specific marine animal but resonates with the essence of oceanic life as a whole. From dolphins to coral reefs to the very currents that flow through the sea, Emily feels as though her spirit belongs to the ocean.

Identification

Emily identifies most closely with marine vertebrates, including fish and mammals like dolphins. Her connection isn't tied to one species but rather the broader family of creatures that call the ocean home.

Experiences and Shifts

- Fluid Shifts: Emily experiences what she calls "fluid shifts," where her mindset and sensations drift from feeling like a dolphin navigating through ocean waves to being a seahorse anchored in a coral garden.
- Composite Shifts: At times, her shifts are composites of different marine animals, feeling both the playfulness of a dolphin and the fluidity of fish swimming in schools.

Rituals and Practices

Emily has a small sanctuary in her home dedicated to her connection with the ocean. It features shells, sand, and seaweed along with pictures and figures of various marine animals. She spends time here meditating, often with ocean sounds playing in the background to help deepen her connection with her oceanic identity.

Challenges

One challenge Emily faces is the lack of specificity in her identification. While some Therians have a specific animal they can deeply research and emulate, Emily's broad identification means she often spreads her attention across various ocean creatures and their ecologies.

Community and Understanding

While Emily faces some misunderstandings within the Therian community due to her broad identification, she has found a few online forums and communities that are open to the complexities of Cladotherianthropy.

4. Contherianthropy

For Contherians, the journey of Therianthropy is not one of fluctuating shifts but of constant oneness with their theriotype. The experience is not episodic; rather, it's an unwavering part of their identity that influences their thoughts, emotions, and actions on a continual basis.

The Nature of the Experience

- Consistency Over Time: Unlike other forms of Therianthropy that involve shifting states, Contherians describe their experience as consistent and unchanging over time.
- Integrated Identity: Contherians often describe their experience as a seamless blend of human and animal traits that exist in harmony rather than conflict.

Living a Contherian Life

- No Shifting: One of the defining characteristics of Contherianthropy is the absence of shifts. While they may have moods or feelings that are influenced by their theriotype, these are not seen as "shifts" but as a natural part of their constant state of being.
- Balanced Perspective: Because their theriotype is a constant part of their identity, many Contherians describe a balanced perspective that takes into account both human and animalistic viewpoints.

Examples of Contherian Behavior

- Alex, the Contherian Wolf: Alex identifies as a wolf and feels this connection consistently, every single day. For Alex, wolf-like traits such as loyalty to a "pack" (friends and family), territoriality, and a preference for open spaces are always present.
- Maria, the Contherian Hawk: Maria feels a continuous connection with hawks. Her keen eye for details, heightened awareness of her surroundings, and love for high places are persistent traits, never shifting or changing with time.

Misunderstandings and Clarifications

- Not 'Lesser': Because their experience lacks shifts, Contherians sometimes face misunderstandings or questions about the "authenticity" of their Therianthropy. However, the lack of shifts doesn't make their experience any less valid; it's simply different.

- Unique Challenges: Contherians may face challenges in explaining their constant state to those accustomed to the more common "shifting" forms of Therianthropy.

Contherianthropy presents a unique, constant experience of animal identity. For Contherians, their non-human identity isn't something that comes and goes but is an integral, steady part of who they are. This contributes to the beautiful tapestry of experiences and identities within the Therian community.

Chapter 2: The Therian Journey

∞ ∞ ∞

"In the footprints of the past, we find the path to our innermost selves, tracing the ancient bonds that unite beast and humankind."

∞ ∞ ∞

The journey to discovering one's Therian identity is as unique as the individuals who undertake it. While some stumble upon the realization early in life, others may take years or even decades to arrive at this understanding. The path is often marked by introspection, personal growth, and a sense of awakening to one's inner nature. This chapter aims to shed light on these deeply personal experiences, highlighting common milestones, and underscoring the importance of self-discovery and acceptance.

Personal Anecdotes and Stories of Discovering One's Therian Identity

The Early Years

In the early years, the whispers of a therian identity often murmur softly in the hearts of the young. Oblivious to their meaning, the echoes of another life – a life led with paws, wings, or fins – hum like a distant melody.

Even in childhood, a therian may sense a unique alignment with the animal kingdom. A child might feel a peculiar kinship with the wolves at the zoo or feel inexplicably at home in the serenity of the forest, resonating with the songs of the birds and the rustle of leaves. They might find themselves unconsciously emulating animal behaviors, a subconscious echo of their inner identity.

Recurring dreams often play a significant role, providing a fantastical escape where the child runs as a cheetah or soars as an eagle. In these dreams, they find a freedom and understanding unattainable in waking life. These nightly journeys often become cherished experiences, awaiting eagerly as the world slumbers.

Despite these early connections, the lack of context and understanding can lead to confusion and a feeling of isolation. Without the vocabulary to express their experiences, these young therians may feel misunderstood, yearning for connection and acceptance.

Nature often becomes a sanctuary for these individuals. The great outdoors, filled with the whispers of ancient times, may offer solace and a sense of belonging. The natural world provides a space for exploration, both of the external world and the internal landscapes of their identity.

As these individuals age, the pieces of the puzzle may begin to fall into place. Encounters with the therian community, literature, and online resources can provide the much-needed context and language to articulate their experiences. This newfound understanding embarks them on a journey of self-acceptance, unveiling the beautiful tapestry of their therian identity.

By recounting these early experiences, the book endeavors to offer a beacon of recognition and understanding for those in the early stages of discovering their therian nature. The stories shed light on the shared experiences of the community, fostering a sense of connection and unity among therians worldwide.

The Catalyst

Every journey has its pivotal moments that tilt the world's axis, causing individuals to see themselves and their place within the universe from a fresh perspective. For many embarking on the journey of Therian discovery, such a catalyst is a significant life event that reverberates deep within their soul, instigating a quest for understanding and alignment.

For some, a profound encounter with the natural world, untouched and raw, can awaken the dormant echoes of their animalistic identity. A solitary walk amidst the ancient whispers of a dense forest or a quiet moment by a babbling stream can stir the inner call of their Therian nature. In these serene instances, a hidden, inner self murmurs, yearning for acknowledgment and exploration.

An unexpected connection with an animal can serve as another powerful catalyst. A gaze shared with a wolf, the graceful flight of an eagle, or the gentle nuzzle of a deer can transcend words, resonating with the soul's uncharted dimensions. These silent conversations may unearth buried truths, guiding individuals toward the revelation of their Therian essence.

Sometimes, the catalyst may be shrouded in the darkness of trauma. Amid the turmoil and tempest of life's challenges, individuals might unearth their inner strength and resilience, reflecting the spirit of their Therian identity. In the crucible of adversity, the awareness of their animalistic kinship whispers support and solidarity, offering a beacon of light and healing.

Propelled by these pivotal moments, individuals often embark on a quest for clarity, insight, and community. The Therian community emerges as a haven of understanding and acceptance amidst the fog of confusion. Here, they find the language to articulate their experiences, the wisdom to navigate the intricacies of their identity, and the fellowship of kindred spirits. The shared narratives within the community weave a tapestry of affirmation and recognition, bolstering the individuals in their journey of Therian exploration and self-discovery.

By delving into the depths of these catalytic experiences, this section aims to illuminate the diverse pathways leading to the awakening of Therian identity, offering guidance, reflection, and companionship to those navigating this sacred journey.

The 'Aha' Moment

In the mosaic of a Therian's journey, the 'Aha' moment shines as a pivotal crystal, reflecting clarity and understanding amidst the exploration of self. This instant is where the scattered pieces of experiences, feelings, and introspections harmoniously converge, unveiling the portrait of their true Therian identity.

For many, this moment blossoms when they stumble upon the word 'Therian.' Within these syllables lies the key that unlocks the language of their soul, offering them the words to express the long-held feelings and inklings nestled within their being. In the discovery of this term, they find a mirror reflecting their true essence, a harmonious alignment of their human and animalistic selves.

The digital realm serves as a beacon, guiding individuals towards the shores of connection and understanding. Online Therian communities emerge as sanctuaries, brimming with shared experiences, wisdom, and support. In these virtual havens, individuals find the freedom to express their Therian identity, basking in the warm embrace of like-minded souls.

The pages of literature on Therianthropy offer another path to the 'Aha' moment. Within the inked words and stories, individuals find echoes of their own journey, resonating with the tales of self-discovery, acceptance, and unity with their animal counterparts. The literature acts as a compass, pointing towards the affirmation and understanding of their Therian identity.

The 'Aha' moment culminates in an overwhelming sense of belonging, a soulful homecoming that transcends the physical realm. In this sublime instant, Therians are enveloped in the recognition of their true self, bathed in the light of self-love, acceptance, and unity with the universal tapestry of Therianthropy. The 'Aha' moment stands as a cherished milestone in their journey, a gentle whisper of their inner truth and the vibrant celebration of their multifaceted identity.

The Importance of Self-Discovery and Acceptance

Internal Acceptance

Internal acceptance in the context of Therianthropy is a pivotal yet intimate journey towards self-understanding and self-love. It's about facing the inner self with honesty, curiosity, and compassion. For many Therians, this path is marked by moments of doubt and confusion as they grapple with the depth of their animalistic identities amidst a predominantly human-oriented society.

Doubt and skepticism are often unwelcome companions on the path to internal acceptance. Therians may question the legitimacy of their feelings and experiences, wondering if they are alone in their unique perceptions. Overcoming these doubts necessitates a robust inner dialogue, self-compassion, and the courage to embrace one's truth unequivocally. As Therians surmount these inner obstacles, the embrace of their animalistic nature unfolds as a powerful and liberating experience. It's an affirmation of their authentic self, a warm embrace of their intrinsic identity. This internal acceptance illuminates the path ahead, enabling Therians to engage with their community and the broader world from a place of confidence, clarity, and self-assuredness.

Reflection and introspection are vital tools in this journey. Through thoughtful self-examination, Therians delve into the layers of their identity, unraveling the threads that weave together their human and animalistic selves. This exploration strengthens their internal foundation, reinforcing their understanding and acceptance of their unique identities as they navigate the multifaceted world of Therianthropy.

In essence, internal acceptance is not a singular event but a continuous process of self-affirmation and self-love. It's about honoring one's Therian identity amidst the cacophony of societal expectations and norms, and standing steadfast in the truth of one's being. This internal harmony cultivates a resilient and vibrant inner world, empowering Therians to embark on their external journey with assurance, strength, and an unwavering sense of self.

External Acceptance

External acceptance for Therians is a significant hurdle, intertwined with societal recognition and understanding. The act of "coming out" as a Therian to friends, family, and society at large is a vulnerable step. Despite the liberation it brings in expressing one's true identity, it can also open doors to scrutiny, misunderstanding, and judgment from others. It's a delicate balance of honesty, risk, and the hopeful expectation of acceptance.

Societal stigmas around Therianthropy persist, often rooted in misconceptions and a lack of knowledge about the community and its members. Therians may confront skepticism, disbelief, and sometimes outright ridicule or hostility when they reveal their identities to others. The path towards societal acceptance involves both individual and collective efforts to educate, inform, and demystify Therianthropy, helping to dispel unfounded stigmas and foster a more inclusive and understanding environment.

Community support plays a crucial role in this aspect of the Therian journey. Within the Therian community, individuals find a space of mutual understanding, shared experience, and empathetic support. This network serves as a foundation from which Therians can navigate the external world, armed with the assurance that they are not alone in their experiences or their quest for acceptance.

Allies, individuals who may not identify as Therian but support and advocate for the community, are also instrumental in advancing external acceptance. By lending their voices, they amplify the message of understanding, inclusion, and respect for Therian identities, helping to bridge the gap between the Therian community and broader society.

Ultimately, the journey towards external acceptance is ongoing, marked by gradual shifts in societal perception, awareness, and understanding. It's a path paved with both challenges and triumphs, each step forward reflecting the resilience, courage, and unwavering commitment of the Therian community to affirm their rightful place in the diverse tapestry of human experience.

In conclusion, while the road to external acceptance is fraught with obstacles, the combined efforts of the Therian community and their allies continuously work towards a future where every Therian can openly and proudly embrace their identity without fear of judgment or exclusion.

Discovering one's Therian identity is a profound journey, laden with milestones that often have deep emotional and psychological significance. While the path to this realization can be long and winding, it is a journey that brings immense personal growth and a richer understanding of oneself. Each story is unique, each experience invaluable, but the overarching theme remains the same: the journey to embrace one's inner nature is a transformative one, and it's a path that many find incredibly rewarding.

In the chapters that follow, we'll dive deeper into the multifaceted world of Therianthropy, exploring the terminology, ethical considerations, community aspects, and much more. This foundation of understanding and acceptance sets the stage for what promises to be an enlightening exploration of Therian experiences and perspectives.

Chapter 3: Therian Terminology and Concepts

∞ ∞ ∞

"In the myriad forms of being, each soul finds its own melody, a unique harmony in the grand symphony of existence."

∞ ∞ ∞

As with any specialized field or community, Therianthropy comes with its own set of terms and concepts that help articulate the diverse range of experiences and perspectives within it. Understanding these terms not only provides valuable insights into the Therian experience but also aids in dispelling misconceptions that often surround it. This chapter aims to clarify important terminology and explore concepts unique to the Therian community.

Important Terms

Theriotype

Theriotype refers to the specific animal a Therian deeply identifies with on a personal and spiritual level. The range of theriotypes is as diverse as the animal kingdom itself, encompassing not only terrestrial, aquatic, and avian species but also, in some instances, creatures of myth and legend. Each Therian's connection to their theriotype is unique and profoundly personal, reflecting various aspects of their inner life, emotions, and spiritual pathway.

Wolves, eagles, and dolphins are common theriotypes, each representing distinct attributes and energies. A wolf theriotype, for example, may signify a strong sense of community and loyalty, while an eagle might symbolize freedom and keen insight, and a dolphin could represent playfulness and intelligence. However, the significance of each theriotype varies for every Therian, as it is a deeply personal association.

Some Therians identify with mythical creatures such as dragons, griffins, or phoenixes. This connection transcends the physical realm, delving into the spiritual, symbolic, and mythical dimensions of identity. These theriotypes can embody a range of meanings, from transformation and rebirth (phoenix) to wisdom and power (dragon), reflecting the multifaceted nature of Therianthropy.

Understanding one's theriotype is an exploratory process. It involves introspection, meditation, and often dialogue with other Therians to gain insight into the nuanced connection between their human existence and animal identity. This understanding is fluid and evolving, mirroring the individual's journey of self-discovery and growth within the context of their Therian identity.

Central to the concept of theriotype is a profound respect for the animal or entity with which one identifies. This respect underpins the Therian's relationship with their theriotype, fostering a deep sense of kinship, understanding, and mutual reverence. It underscores the essential interconnectedness of all beings, reinforcing the intrinsic value and dignity of every creature, real or mythical, within the grand tapestry of life.

In essence, the theriotype is a vital facet of Therian identity, offering a window into the soul's landscape, reflecting inner desires, fears, strengths, and aspirations. It serves as a guide, companion, and mirror on the Therian's ongoing journey of exploration, understanding, and self-acceptance.

Awakening

The term "Awakening" in the context of Therianthropy refers to the enlightening period or event wherein individuals uncover and acknowledge their Therian identity. It's a paramount experience, a significant milestone on the path of self-discovery and acceptance.

The Awakening can manifest as a sudden, pivotal moment of clarity, akin to a lightning bolt of understanding. For others, it unfolds gradually, a slow dawning of awareness and identification with a specific animal or entity. Both pathways offer unique challenges and insights as individuals navigate the complexities of their emerging identities.

This period can be emotionally charged, accompanied by confusion, excitement, fear, and joy. The fluctuation of emotions is a natural aspect of the awakening journey, reflecting the internal shifts and alignments occurring within the individual. The emotional turbulence gradually gives way to a more profound understanding and acceptance of their Therian nature, forging a path to internal harmony and self-acceptance.

Awakening often propels individuals to seek further knowledge about Therianthropy, leading them to engage with online forums, communities, and resources that provide guidance and support during this transitional period. Engaging with the Therian community offers opportunities for individuals to share their experiences, gain insights, and find validation for their feelings and self-understanding.

The Awakening is not just about identifying as a Therian; it's a profound journey of personal growth and self-exploration. It is about learning to embrace the multifaceted aspects of one's identity, accepting both human and animalistic elements, and finding a harmonious balance between the two. The process fosters resilience, self-love, and a deeper connection with the self and the broader Therian community.

In essence, the Awakening is a fundamental and transformative experience in the life of a Therian, marking the passage from uncertainty to self-awareness, from confusion to clarity, and from self-doubt to self-acceptance. It's a beautiful, sometimes challenging journey that ultimately enriches the individual's life, offering a fuller, more nuanced understanding of themselves and their place in the world.

Shifts

In the realm of Therianthropy, the term 'shifts' refers to the transient states wherein individuals intensely feel their animal traits come to the foreground. It's a predominant feature of the Therian experience, providing a more profound connection to their theriotype.

Types of Shifts
1. Mental Shifts (M-shifts):
Characterized by a change in mindset to that of the theriotype.
May experience instincts, thoughts, and emotions resembling their identified animal.

2. Phantom Shifts (P-shifts):
Involve sensation of non-human physical features.
A tail, wings, or claws may be felt but not seen.

3. Sensory Shifts (S-shifts):
Heightened senses mirroring their theriotype.
Enhanced hearing, smell, or vision may occur.

4. Astral Shifts:
Occur within spiritual or astral planes.
May manifest as the theriotype during meditations or spiritual explorations.

The experience of shifting varies widely among Therians. Some describe it as voluntary, while others view it as an uncontrollable phenomenon, spontaneously occurring in response to specific triggers, emotions, or environments.

Shifts can encompass an extensive emotional and psychological spectrum, offering both challenges and enlightenment. Individuals might grapple with the abrupt and sometimes overwhelming surge of animalistic instincts and sensations, necessitating adaptation and understanding. The experience, while intense, often fortifies the bond between Therians and their theriotypes, deepening their insight into their dual existence.

In navigating shifts, the Therian community stands as a beacon of support and guidance. Sharing experiences, exchanging coping strategies, and mutual understanding foster a supportive environment for individuals to explore and understand their shifts comprehensively.

In essence, shifts are pivotal to the Therian experience, nurturing self-awareness, exploration, and a profound bond with their theriotype. As individuals traverse the landscape of their shifts, they emerge with heightened understanding, resilience, and a deeper connection to their inner selves and the expansive Therian community.

Howls

A 'Howl' is an in-person gathering organized within the Therian community, aimed at creating a shared space for Therians to connect, share their journeys, experiences, and insights, and express their theriotypes in a supportive and understanding environment.

The Purpose of Howls
Building Community:
Howls help in strengthening the sense of community among Therians. It's an opportunity for individuals to meet others with similar experiences, exchange stories, offer advice, and provide emotional support.

Expressing Theriotypes:
Attendees are encouraged to freely express their theriotypes through various group activities. This collective expression allows Therians to immerse themselves in their theriotypes, promoting understanding, acceptance, and unity within the community.

Sharing Knowledge:
Howls often include discussions and workshops covering diverse aspects of Therianthropy, such as navigating shifts, understanding awakening, and fostering both internal and external acceptance.

Activities at Howls

Group Discussions:
Engage in group conversations about Therianthropy, share personal stories of awakening and shifts, and discuss challenges and successes.

Nature Excursions:
Embark on group outings to natural settings, allowing Therians to connect with nature, their theriotypes, and each other.

Expressive Arts:
Participate in activities like art, dance, and music that allow for creative expression of their theriotype.

Meditation Sessions:
Join in guided meditation focusing on deepening the connection to their theriotype and understanding their shifts.

The Impact of Howls
Howls contribute significantly to individual and communal growth within the Therian community. They offer a space for Therians to feel understood, accepted, and celebrated in their unique identities. The experiences and connections made at Howls continue to resonate with participants long after the gathering, reinforcing their sense of self and their place within the Therian community.

In the world of Therianthropy, Howls stand as vital congregations that echo the values of unity, understanding, and mutual support, aiding individuals in their continuous journey of self-exploration and acceptance within the realm of their therian identities.

Clarification of Common Misconceptions

Therianthropy is Not a Choice
One of the most pervasive misconceptions is that being a Therian is a lifestyle choice. However, most Therians would affirm that their identity is an intrinsic part of who they are, not something they opted into.

Therians are Not Delusional
Another misconception is that Therians are delusional or suffering from a psychological disorder. While Therianthropy can have psychological aspects, it is generally not considered a disorder by the community.

Therianthropy vs. Furry Fandom
Therians are often confused with Furries, but the two are distinct. Furries are enthusiasts of anthropomorphic animals and do not necessarily identify as an animal, whereas Therians have a deep-seated identification with a specific animal or animals.

The Difference Between Therianthropy and Other Related Concepts

Therianthropy vs. Otherkin
While both communities involve a form of identification beyond being human, Otherkin often identify with mythical or fantastical beings like dragons, elves, or even celestial bodies. Therians usually identify with existent, earthly animals.

Therianthropy and Spirituality
Though Therianthropy can be a spiritual experience for some, it is not tied to any particular religious belief or spiritual practice. It is an identity and experience that can exist independently of religious or spiritual views.

Understanding the terminology and concepts specific to Therianthropy is crucial for a comprehensive grasp of what it means to be a Therian. With a rich lexicon that captures the nuances of various experiences, Therians can better communicate, relate, and find community. Equally important is the role of this vocabulary in clarifying misconceptions, thereby fostering a more accepting and informed society.

Chapter 4: The Role of Community

∞ ∞ ∞

"In the gathering of like spirits, we find not only acceptance and understanding but also the reflection of our own inner worlds."

∞ ∞ ∞

Community plays a pivotal role in the life of a Therian, offering a sense of belonging and understanding that is often hard to find elsewhere. This chapter delves into the significance of having a supportive network, the role of online forums and communities, and the importance of real-world gatherings, often referred to as "howls."

Importance of Having a Support Network

Emotional Support

In the diverse world of Therianthropy, emotional support holds paramount significance. Therians, like any other individuals, seek understanding, acceptance, and a space where they can freely express their authentic selves. The journey of living as a Therian, while rich and rewarding, may often tread the path of isolation and misunderstanding, especially when surrounded by individuals unaware or unreceptive to this unique identity. This solitude can cast shadows of doubt, confusion, and emotional turmoil.

A supportive community emerges as a beacon of hope in such times, knitting a web of connections and shared experiences. It stands as a testament to the unity and diversity within the Therian community, offering a safe harbor where individuals can navigate the waters of their identities without the fear of ridicule or judgment. Here, stories are shared, wisdom is exchanged, and the threads of understanding weave a warm, embracing tapestry of support.

In these nurturing environments, Therians can explore the depths of their identities, understanding the facets that make them unique and learning the intricacies of their theriotypes. The emotional safety net that a compassionate community provides is indispensable, granting Therians the confidence to walk their paths with pride, assurance, and a cherished sense of belonging. This fortifying emotional support lays the cornerstone for a robust Therian journey, enabling individuals to flourish in their truth and bask in the collective warmth of like-minded souls.

Validation and Affirmation

In the vast realm of Therianthropy, the quest for validation and affirmation is a fundamental human need. The community plays a crucial role in fulfilling this need, offering a sanctuary where Therians can find resonance with their experiences and emotions. This resonance echoes the shared harmonies of lived experiences, interwoven in the diverse tapestry of the Therian journey.

In a world where mainstream understanding and acceptance of Therianthropy are still budding, the community emerges as a robust pillar, bolstering the spirits of Therians as they navigate the intricate pathways of their unique identities. Within the embrace of this communal bond, Therians find the freedom to delve into discussions about their shifts, explore the landscape of their theriotypes, and unravel the complex threads that embroider their Therian identities.

This open dialogue fosters a vibrant environment of mutual affirmation, where the echoes of shared stories reverberate, weaving a melodic symphony of understanding and acceptance. The community blossoms as a garden of validation, where each Therian, with their distinctive hues and patterns, contributes to the beautiful mosaic of collective identity. In this garden, the seeds of self-awareness and self-acceptance take root, nurtured by the nourishing rays of affirmation and the enriching soil of communal support.

Through this journey of collective validation and affirmation, Therians embolden each other to stride confidently on the path of self-discovery and growth. As they traverse this path, the guiding lights of community and mutual support illuminate the way, dispelling the shadows of doubt and uncertainty, and bathing their journey in the luminous glow of acceptance and understanding.

Knowledge Sharing

In the Therian community, the exchange of diverse ideas, personal experiences, and practical insights is paramount, knitting a robust web of mutual understanding and support. Knowledge sharing within the community emerges as a beacon that sheds light on the multifaceted aspects of Therian life.

The communal platform allows Therians to disseminate and receive valuable information about navigating the intricate realms of their identities. The dialogue that ensues within this supportive framework enables individuals to delve deeper into the understanding of their theriotypes, shifts, and various other dimensions of Therianthropy. It allows for a continual flow of wisdom and insight, aiding individuals in managing and embracing their Therian identities with confidence and clarity.

Therians from different walks of life, each harboring a wealth of personal experiences and unique perspectives, contribute to this enriching reservoir of knowledge. This diversity blossoms into a vibrant garden of insight, offering guidance and support to those navigating the path of Therianthropy. Discussions within the community span a myriad of topics, from exploring the nature of individual theriotypes and understanding the dynamics of shifts to sharing practical advice for 'coming out' as a Therian and fostering external acceptance.

This synergistic exchange within the Therian community fortifies the bonds of mutual support and understanding, further solidifying the foundation upon which individuals can confidently embrace and celebrate their unique identities. The shared knowledge within the community not only enlightens but also empowers Therians, imbuing them with the strength and clarity to navigate the journey of life with unwavering assurance and a profound sense of self-awareness.

Being part of a community facilitates the exchange of information, advice, and practical tips for managing life as a Therian.

Online Forums and Communities

Virtual Safe Spaces

In the expansive realm of the digital world, Therians find solace and connection in virtual safe spaces. Online forums, social media groups, and other digital platforms emerge as sanctuaries for individuals exploring or embracing their Therian identities. These digital domains offer a shelter of understanding, acceptance, and camaraderie, transcending geographical barriers and uniting Therians from all corners of the globe in a shared journey of self-discovery and affirmation.

For many who are newly awakened to their Therian identity, these online spaces often serve as the initial beacon of guidance and support. They find a world where their experiences are echoed, their feelings validated, and their identities celebrated. The virtual realm provides a platform for the fledgling Therian to engage in enriching dialogues, seek answers to pressing questions, and navigate the path of acceptance and understanding alongside seasoned members of the community.

Beyond the exchange of knowledge and insights, these virtual spaces foster a sense of belonging and community. In a world where misunderstanding and stigma might cloud their daily lives, Therians find in these online platforms a refuge of mutual respect and affirmation. They are environments where individuals can express their theriotypes freely, discuss their shifts, and share their awakening stories without the fear of judgment or ridicule.

In essence, these virtual safe spaces act as lighthouses in the vast ocean of the internet, guiding Therians towards a community where their unique identities are understood, respected, and celebrated. Here, amidst the warmth of communal connection, Therians are empowered to flourish and thrive, basking in the glow of shared understanding and unwavering support.

Online forums and social media platforms have given Therians from around the world a place to connect. These virtual spaces are often the first point of contact for those newly awakened to their Therian identity.

Anonymity and Openness

In the virtual realms of forums and social media, the veil of anonymity stands as a guardian of freedom and openness for Therians worldwide. It crafts a space where individuals can unravel the layers of their experiences, fears, questions, and insights without the weight of real-world judgment, scrutiny, or misunderstanding. This anonymity blossoms as a precious boon for those still navigating the delicate paths of their Therian identity, permitting a freedom of expression often unattainable in their physical worlds.

Within these digital boundaries, Therians find a stage where their voices echo without restraint. They can delve into profound conversations, share the intimacies of their shifts and awakenings, and seek the counsel of fellow Therians with an honesty often muted by the uncertainties of societal acceptance. The anonymity of online platforms opens doors to a sanctuary where the complexities of Therian experiences can unfurl in all their authenticity, fostering a collective comprehension and mutual respect among community members.

But even beyond the liberation of anonymous expression, these platforms subtly lay the bricks for the bridge to openness. As Therians intertwine in the dance of shared experience and mutual support, the fears and doubts that may shroud their everyday lives begin to dissipate. The online world, bathed in the light of anonymity, nurtures the seeds of confidence and self-acceptance, enabling individuals to carry the torch of their Therian identity into the realms of their external, everyday existence, fortifying the bonds of the global Therian community.

The Role of Moderators and Admins

The heartbeat of online Therian communities, moderators and administrators, or "mods and admins," bear the responsibility of nurturing and safeguarding the delicate ecosystem of virtual safe spaces. They stand as sentinels, ensuring the environment remains supportive, inclusive, and respectful. Their role transcends mere oversight, emerging as the custodians of community wellbeing.

Moderators and admins create the framework for constructive conversation, steering the dialogue to foster learning, validation, and mutual support. Their presence helps to diffuse tension and resolve conflicts, maintaining the harmony essential for the community's growth and the well-being of its members. In the dynamic world of online interactions, their adept management helps in navigating the diverse personalities, opinions, and emotions that naturally converge, ensuring every voice finds a listening ear without the clutter of negativity.

By enforcing guidelines and fostering a culture of respect and empathy, these community leaders ensure that the exchange of knowledge and experiences occurs seamlessly. They facilitate the delicate balance of anonymity and openness, allowing members to share their journeys, insights, and challenges in an environment where they feel seen, heard, and protected.

Their contribution extends to providing resources, information, and guidance to those in search of understanding their Therian identity. They link individuals to networks, literature, and experts, broadening the avenues for exploration and learning. Through their dedicated efforts, moderators and admins reinforce the foundations of online Therian communities, making them resilient havens for those seeking connection, understanding, and support in their Therian journey.

Therian Gatherings and Howls

What Happens at a Howl

A Therian howl is an in-person gathering where Therians can meet, share experiences, and often engage in activities that allow them to express their theriotypes. It is mentioned in our previous chapter for more.

The Importance of Real-World Interaction

While online communities provide much-needed support and information, nothing can replace the experience of meeting other Therians face-to-face. Real-world interactions provide a level of connection and understanding that is hard to replicate online.

Precautions and Best Practices

While howls are generally positive experiences, it's important to take certain precautions. These can include ensuring the gathering is well-organized, public enough to be safe, and respectful of local laws and customs.

The community is not just a peripheral aspect of being a Therian; it's often central to the Therian experience itself. Whether online or in person, these communal spaces offer Therians the emotional support, validation, and practical advice that help them navigate life with this unique identity. The community serves as both a sanctuary and a resource, enriching the lives of Therians in countless ways.

Chapter 5: Everyday Life as a Therian

∞ ∞ ∞

"Each day is a step through the wilderness of life, where the therian spirit guides and empowers our journey."

∞ ∞ ∞

Navigating everyday life as a Therian involves a balance of challenges and benefits. This identity not only adds complexity to ordinary activities but also enriches them, bringing about a unique set of experiences and viewpoints. In this chapter, we delve into the highs and lows of daily life as a Therian, share stories of individuals who have found a harmonious balance, and offer practical tips on incorporating Therian traits into everyday living.

Challenges and Benefits

Social Stigma and Misunderstanding

The journey of a Therian is shadowed by the cold veil of societal misunderstanding and stigma. In a world that often clings to the binary, the transcendent nature of a Therian identity dances beyond the familiar borders, making it a subject of skepticism and sometimes, ridicule. This societal reluctance to embrace the diverse spectra of identity propels many Therians into a silence woven with caution and secrecy.

Therians, facing unwarranted assumptions and judgments, often bear the weight of misinterpretation. The world's unfamiliarity with the depth and legitimacy of their experiences and identities thrusts them into the outskirts of societal validation, leaving them to navigate the turbulent seas of isolation and self-doubt.

This secrecy, a forced armor against the sharp edges of societal prejudice, often adds an additional layer of struggle to the Therian journey. The yearning to unfurl one's true self in the broad daylight of acceptance is met with the harsh winds of misunderstanding and dismissal. It underscores the essential need for internal fortitude and the support of a community that mirrors their truth and echoes their voices against the stony walls of societal stigmas.

In the battle against these societal challenges, education emerges as a potent weapon. Raising awareness and dispelling myths about Therianthropy illuminates the path towards societal understanding, acceptance, and the dissipation of unfounded stigmas, allowing Therians to stand unshielded, their identities resplendent in the light of acknowledgment and respect.

Sensory Overwhelm

For many Therians, a heightened sensitivity is not just a mere occurrence; it's a vivid tapestry of their daily lives, painting their interactions with the world in bold, intense strokes. This acute sensory awareness can translate into an overwhelming influx of sensory information, making certain environments or situations a complex labyrinth of stimuli.

Imagine walking into a bustling space, where each color, sound, and scent is magnified, echoing with an intensity that drowns the senses in a torrent of information. For some

Therians, this is their reality, a realm where the sensory world unfurls with an overwhelming vibrancy.

This heightened sensory experience, while offering a rich and profound interaction with the world, carries with it the potential for sensory overwhelm. Situations that many navigate with ease become a tumultuous sea of stimuli for Therians, with waves of sensory information crashing against the shores of their perception. Loud environments can escalate into a cacophony that drowns out thought, while bright or fluctuating lights can paint the world in a dizzying mosaic of confusion.

Understanding and navigating this sensory overwhelm is an integral aspect of life for many Therians. It involves the cultivation of coping strategies and the carving out of sensory-safe spaces. These adaptations not only provide respite from the sensory storm but also offer a haven where Therians can embrace the richness of their sensory world, unburdened by overwhelm, and cradled in the embrace of understanding and acceptance.

Emotional Enrichment

For many Therians, a heightened sensitivity is not just a mere occurrence; it's a vivid tapestry of their daily lives, painting their interactions with the world in bold, intense strokes. This acute sensory awareness can translate into an overwhelming influx of sensory information, making certain environments or situations a complex labyrinth of stimuli.

Imagine walking into a bustling space, where each color, sound, and scent is magnified, echoing with an intensity that drowns the senses in a torrent of information. For some Therians, this is their reality, a realm where the sensory world unfurls with an overwhelming vibrancy.

This heightened sensory experience, while offering a rich and profound interaction with the world, carries with it the potential for sensory overwhelm. Situations that many navigate with ease become a tumultuous sea of stimuli for Therians, with waves of sensory information crashing against the shores of their perception. Loud environments can escalate into a cacophony that drowns out thought, while bright or fluctuating lights can paint the world in a dizzying mosaic of confusion.

Understanding and navigating this sensory overwhelm is an integral aspect of life for many Therians. It involves the cultivation of coping strategies and the carving out of sensory-safe spaces. These adaptations not only provide respite from the sensory storm but also offer a haven where Therians can embrace the richness of their sensory world, unburdened by overwhelm, and cradled in the embrace of understanding and acceptance.

Despite the challenges, many Therians report that their unique identity provides a deep sense of emotional richness and fulfillment, transforming even mundane activities into deeply engaging experiences.

Stories of Living a Balanced Life

Interview with a Real life Therian: Thorn (Therian Territory)

In the course of researching for this book, we were given the exceptional opportunity to connect with and interview a real-life therian, known by the name of Thorn. Thorn is not just any therian, but one who has made a significant mark in the online community, contributing a wealth of knowledge, experiences, and support through popular platforms like YouTube and Discord under the name of "Therian Territory".

Below is the unedited transcript of our conversation with Thorn, allowing readers to gain unfiltered insight into his journey, challenges, and the impact of his therian identity on various aspects of his life.

1. Can you share your awakening journey as a therian?

Thorn: So as a kid I always considered myself to be a nature-being so to speak. I felt a disconnect from other humans, and had early wolf-like experiences such as strongly thinking in wolf hierarchies, enjoying play fighting and chasing a lot, and smaller things such as food possessions. There was a girl, also a therian, who seemed to be just like me. When I was with her, I was able to bring out that wolf side of myself. Up till the age of 18, I felt no need to actually define what I experienced, I was happy being a wolf with her. But when we started losing contact with one another, I didn't want to lose connection with my wolf side as well. So I actively began digging on the internet for people who experience animal behaviour like me. I eventually found the therian community, as therianthropy seemed to describe my experience to the T. That's when I sort of "awakened" as a therian, yet I had known I was a wolf for a long time.

2. How has identifying as a therian impacted your daily life and relationships?

Thorn: It does have a daily impact for sure. That disconnect I have from humans has always stayed, which causes a lot of species dysphoria for me. While everyone can have loads of fun hanging out together, I tend to long to be out in the woods relaxing instead, and so forth. I have found fellow alterhumans in my area, which has created beautiful friendships and I am even in a relationship with an Otherkin. I find that I can read and communicate with these people way more easily, as they seem to experience the same type of behaviour, connection with nature, and disconnect from other humans like I do. It's almost as if they speak my language. So while I am able to get by in my daily life just fine, species dysphoria and feeling distant from other humans will always be a struggle, some days more than others.

3. What are some misconceptions people have about therians, and what would you like them to know?

Thorn: There MANY misconceptions. It kind of depends on what group of people you are referring to. People who know nothing of it all will often see therianthropy as either the same as furry (which is not at all related), the same as having a spirit animal/totem (which also isn't the same as a theriotype is not distinct from yourself, plus this is heavily appropriating from the native americans), or they believe we're just kids doing quadrobics on Tiktok (because tbh that's the representation the community mostly has nowadays unfortunately). Within the community itself, there's often the misconception that it is a spiritual belief (it is not inherently spiritual, plus it's an identity and not just a belief). People often also think that it's inherently thinking you have a past life, which also does not describe therianthropy in any way. Therianthropy means you non-physically identify as an animalistic being based on involuntary animalistic experiences. Nothing more, nothing less.

4. Could you describe any challenges you've faced and how you've overcome them?

Thorn: Not directly from being a therian other than the species dysphoria and disconnect from humans I already described. I would say that being bullied as a kid and suffering from social anxiety disorder for most of my life was also indirectly of being a therian, though I wouldn't blame it on that fully either.

5. How does your therian identity influence your spiritual or philosophical beliefs?

Thorn: Though my therianthropy is mostly psychological, I do believe it has allowed me to look at the world through very open minded and nonhuman eyes. I am a pantheist, meaning that I believe every source of energy comes from one source, which is usually called mother earth, or Gaia if you will. Being a therian has mostly made me believe that I have a certain purpose in life. That I should share the views I have of the world with humans, or that I help undo the harms that humans have created in this world.

6. Are there any communities or resources that have been particularly helpful or supportive for you?

Thorn: At the beginning I mostly watched PD's video to help learn about the therian terminology. After that, I have actually mostly created my own spaces, given my YouTube channel and all. I have a Discord server with over 3500 members, which is a great space for me to chat about my experiences. But going to irl therian meetups and hanging out with therian friends has also been insanely beneficial for my mental health. Instagram is also a good space for me to express myself.

Real life example:

Born in Ireland and awakened in her early 20s, Lady ventured into a journey towards self-understanding as she experienced an "other" feeling. At 13, a profound shift in demeanor alarmed both her and her boyfriend. This inexplicable sensation, alien and unsettling, led her down a path of confusion and fear. Initial misconceptions suggested she might be a "furry," but this idea was quickly discarded in distaste. Despite her firm atheistic beliefs, a hesitant exploration into the world of therianthropy began, albeit with limited internet access and a barrage of misinformation.

Upon her deep personal introspection, meditation played a crucial role, helping her connect with her Eastern Canadian Wolf identity. Although her awakening brought moments of societal and personal discord, it illuminated her path to self-acceptance and self-awareness. The journey wasn't devoid of trials; relationships strained and broke under the weight of her therian identity. Friends and family, unaware or unaccepting, contributed to feelings of isolation.

Nevertheless, her relentless pursuit for balance and understanding persevered. Therianthropy instilled in her a deep, instinctive insight, aiding her in navigating the complexities of life. In the embrace of a loving and accepting partner, Lady found solace, love, and a harmonious blend of her human and wolf identities. The journey continues, marked by growth, acceptance, and an unwavering embrace of her true self.

How to Incorporate Therian Traits into Everyday Living

Creating Personal Rituals

Embracing a Therian identity involves more than just internal and external recognition; it also entails integrating this aspect of oneself into the fabric of everyday life. One significant pathway for this integration is through the creation of personal rituals. These structured, repeated activities provide a space for Therians to connect deeply with their theriotypes, fostering a sense of harmony, balance, and attuned self-awareness.

Morning Meditations
Starting the day with a morning meditation can set a tone of inner connectivity and mindfulness. Therians may choose to focus on their theriotype during this time, visualizing themselves embodying the traits, strengths, and spirit of their inner animal. This practice not only helps to cultivate a sense of inner peace and alignment but also strengthens the bond between the Therian and their theriotype, making it a tangible and enriching part of their daily experience.

Nightly Journaling
Nightly journaling serves as another potent ritual for Therians. It provides a dedicated time to reflect on the day's experiences, feelings, and shifts. Writing about these aspects can offer insight, clarity, and a deeper understanding of one's Therian identity and its interplay with the myriad facets of life. Journaling also serves as a historical record, charting the growth, challenges, and triumphs along the Therian journey.

Connecting with Nature
For many Therians, nature holds a special place of resonance and restoration. Creating rituals that involve spending time in nature—whether it's a weekly hike, a daily walk, or periodic camping trips—can facilitate a deeper connection with their theriotype and the natural world. It offers a space to unwind, recharge, and embrace the fullness of their Therian identity in a supportive and nurturing environment.

Creating personal rituals is not about rigid structures or complex activities; it's about carving out time and space to honor, explore, and integrate the Therian identity into daily life. These rituals serve as a gentle, consistent reminder of the richness of the Therian experience, fostering a life of balance, understanding, and profound connection with one's inner animal and the world at large.

Sensory Mindfulness

For Therians experiencing heightened sensory perception, navigating the sensory influx in daily life can sometimes feel overwhelming. This is where the practice of sensory mindfulness becomes essential, transforming potential sensory overload into a nuanced, balanced awareness that enhances life's texture, depth, and resonance.

Understanding Sensory Overwhelm
It's crucial for Therians to understand their sensory boundaries and triggers for overwhelm. This self-awareness forms the foundation for developing effective mindfulness strategies. Recognizing the signs of sensory overload early allows for timely intervention and self-care, mitigating stress and enhancing overall well-being.

Practising Mindfulness
Engaging in mindfulness practices enables Therians to cultivate a centred, balanced state of mind. Techniques such as focused breathing, meditation, and mindfulness-based stress reduction (MBSR) can help manage heightened sensory experiences. By grounding themselves in the present moment, Therians can navigate their enhanced sensory landscape with grace and adaptability.

Sensory Mindfulness Techniques
Therians can develop specific mindfulness techniques tailored to their sensory experiences. For instance, for those with heightened auditory sensitivity, practices such as sound

meditation can help fine-tune their auditory focus, turning potential overwhelm into a deep appreciation for sound's richness and variety.

Similarly, mindful eating practices can transform the experience for those with enhanced taste and smell, turning meal times into a journey of flavour and aroma exploration, rather than a source of overwhelm.

By honing sensory mindfulness, Therians not only manage and mitigate sensory challenges but also enrich their sensory experiences. They can delve deeper into the world's sensory tapestry, savouring subtleties, nuances, and layers that might be overlooked. This practice enhances their connection to the world, their theriotype, and themselves, converting potential challenges into profound assets for personal growth and exploration.

In conclusion, sensory mindfulness stands as a vital tool for Therians with heightened senses, fostering balance, understanding, and a deep, enriching engagement with the sensory world.

Social Navigation

Navigating social situations as a Therian can be a nuanced experience. Here is an in-depth look at managing social circumstances where Therian traits might either aid or obstruct interaction, particularly focusing on the utility of keen observational skills.

Leveraging Observational Skills

Many Therians possess heightened observational skills, akin to the animals they identify with. This acute sense of awareness can be a significant advantage in various social settings. For example, during meetings or social gatherings, Therians can use their observational prowess to read the room efficiently, understanding unspoken cues and emotions that many might miss. This ability allows for more empathetic and effective communication, as Therians can tailor their interactions based on the moods and responses of those around them.

Addressing Misunderstandings

However, the journey isn't always smooth. Therians might find themselves misunderstood by people unfamiliar with Therianthropy. In such cases, it's crucial to have a prepared strategy for explaining one's identity in a concise and non-defensive manner. Clear and calm communication can help in alleviating confusion and fostering understanding.

Balancing Therian Traits

In circumstances where Therian traits might hinder social interaction, developing coping and management strategies is essential. If certain environments or situations feel overwhelming due to heightened senses, Therians can plan ahead to minimize discomfort. This could include carrying noise-cancelling headphones for auditory sensitivity or preparing polite exit strategies from overwhelming social engagements.

Ensuring Mutual Respect
At the heart of social navigation lies the principle of mutual respect. Even in the face of curiosity or skepticism from others, maintaining a demeanor of respect and openness fosters positive dialogue and understanding. It's a two-way street—while Therians seek acceptance and understanding from society, offering the same in return is equally crucial.

In conclusion, adept social navigation as a Therian involves leveraging the strengths of one's Therian traits while also having strategies in place to manage potential challenges. This balance ensures not just personal comfort and well-being but also the nurturing of understanding and respect in all social interactions.

The experience of being a Therian permeates every aspect of daily life, from work and social interactions to personal hobbies and family activities. While there are undeniable challenges, the benefits often outweigh them, leading to a life that is emotionally rich and uniquely fulfilling. By learning to incorporate Therian traits effectively, one can not only navigate the complexities of daily life but also enrich it in meaningful ways.

Chapter 6: Navigating Relationships

∞ ∞ ∞

"In the dance of relationships, the therian soul moves with grace, finding connection in the shared rhythm of life."

∞ ∞ ∞

Relationships form the cornerstone of human experience, and for Therians, these interactions carry their own unique nuances. Whether it's the romance that kindles between two souls, the deep bond of friendship, or the complexities of family dynamics, relationships offer both challenges and opportunities for those who identify as Therians. This chapter aims to guide you through the labyrinth of relationships from a Therian perspective.

Romantic Relationships

The Double-Edged Sword of Intimacy

For a Therian, delving into the realm of romantic relationships often unfolds as a journey of vulnerability, understanding, and mutual acceptance. The intricacies of their unique identities necessitate a deeper layer of openness that may not always be easy to navigate.

The Gift of Understanding
One of the bright facets of intimacy in a Therian's relationship is the potential for a deeper understanding and acceptance from their partner. In the best scenarios, a loving partner provides a safe harbor for expression, offering a space for Therians to be their most authentic selves without the fear of judgment or misunderstanding. This understanding lays the foundation for a robust, supportive relationship where both parties flourish.

Vulnerability: A Challenging Landscape
Despite the potential for profound understanding, the path to intimacy also traverses the terrain of vulnerability. Sharing one's Therian identity with a partner involves exposing a core aspect of oneself that might be met with skepticism, confusion, or even disbelief. This emotional exposure can feel daunting for many Therians, especially those who have faced judgment or stigmatization in other areas of their lives.

Navigating Emotional Complexity
The mixed emotions encompassing the desire for intimacy and the fear of vulnerability necessitate adept emotional navigation. Communication emerges as a paramount tool in this journey, allowing both partners to express their feelings, concerns, and questions openly. Through honest dialogue, couples can work together to build a relationship founded on mutual respect, understanding, and acceptance.

Embracing the Duality
In conclusion, while the path to intimacy for a Therian is marked with both rewards and challenges, embracing this duality allows for the cultivation of deeply enriching, supportive relationships. The openness to vulnerability, coupled with clear communication and mutual respect, paves the way for a relationship where both partners are celebrated in their unique individuality.

Disclosing Your Identity

In the complex world of interpersonal relationships, disclosing one's Therian identity stands as a significant milestone, marked by a blend of anticipation, anxiety, and hope. The unveiling of this profound aspect of self carries the potential to either deepen the relational bond or, conversely, introduce tension and misunderstanding.

Timing is Everything
The decision on when to disclose a Therian identity is paramount. It's a deeply personal revelation that requires a supportive and receptive environment. Therians often find it most appropriate to share their identity in the context of a trusting, established relationship where mutual respect and understanding have already been affirmed.

Assessing the Relationship Landscape
Before making the disclosure, it's essential to gauge the potential receptivity of the partner. It's worthwhile to consider their general outlook on Therianthropy and related topics, their openness to diverse identities, and their capacity for empathy and understanding. This assessment can help in preparing for the conversation and anticipating possible responses.

Managing Varied Reactions
Reactions to the disclosure of a Therian identity can span a wide spectrum, from supportive acceptance to confusion, curiosity, or even disbelief. It's crucial for Therians to approach the conversation with clarity, patience, and the readiness to answer questions and provide further insights into their identity. Offering resources, such as literature or online communities, can aid in enhancing understanding.

Navigating Challenges
In instances where the revelation leads to strain or discord in the relationship, it's vital to maintain open lines of communication. Addressing concerns, dispelling misconceptions, and underscoring the significance of this aspect of one's identity can contribute to resolving issues and fostering a stronger relationship bond.

Fostering Mutual Understanding
Ultimately, the disclosure of a Therian identity within a romantic relationship is an avenue to deeper mutual understanding, empathy, and connection. Approaching the situation with sensitivity, openness, and a commitment to communication can pave the way for a strengthened bond, enriched by the embrace of each individual's unique identity.

Compatibility and Shared Experiences

Navigating the intricate landscape of relationships as a Therian brings forth unique challenges and opportunities. One such aspect revolves around the role of shared experiences and compatibility in enriching partnerships.

The Power of Shared Experiences
Shared experiences, especially concerning Therian identity, hold the potential to significantly enhance the depth and understanding within a relationship. Engaging with a partner who resonates with or shares the intricacies of Therianthropy facilitates a profound level of connection and empathy. This shared understanding can be a bedrock for mutual support, open communication, and a deep emotional bond.

Beyond the Therian Community
While the comfort of shared experiences holds undeniable allure, it's also important to acknowledge the richness of diversity in relationships. Being a Therian does not inherently limit one's dating sphere exclusively to the Therian community. Relationships thrive on mutual respect, understanding, and love, transcending the boundaries of shared experiences.

Navigating Differences
In relationships where one partner is a Therian while the other is not, the emphasis shifts to communication, empathy, and mutual respect. It's essential to foster a space where both partners feel heard, understood, and valued in their unique identities and experiences. Navigating these differences with sensitivity and openness can lead to a strengthened, resilient partnership enriched by the amalgamation of diverse perspectives.

Balancing Compatibility and Diversity
In the quest for compatibility and shared experiences within a relationship, it's vital to strike a balance. Embracing shared Therian experiences provides a robust foundation of understanding and connection. Simultaneously, celebrating and navigating the diversity of identity and experience within a partnership contribute to its growth, resilience, and depth, culminating in a rich, multifaceted relationship landscape.

Friendships

The Importance of a Supportive Circle
In the world of a Therian, the strength and understanding embedded in a supportive friendship network hold immeasurable value. The journey of Therianthropy, filled with its unique joys and challenges, underscores the critical need for a robust, empathetic social circle.

A Safe Harbor
For many Therians, friends act as a safe harbor, a place where they can unabashedly be themselves. In these bonds, they find the freedom to express their Therian identity without the fear of judgment or misunderstanding. This level of acceptance and support serves as a bedrock, allowing individuals to navigate the world with greater confidence and assurance.

Emotional Sustenance
A friend who recognizes and honors one's Therian identity contributes significantly to emotional wellbeing. These relationships offer a space for sharing experiences, exploring facets of one's identity, and seeking guidance and empathy in times of uncertainty or difficulty. The emotional sustenance derived from such connections bolsters mental and emotional health, providing a buffer against the potential isolating aspects of life as a Therian.

Navigating Challenges
Therians, like anyone else, face life's myriad challenges. However, with the added layer of navigating societal perceptions and misunderstandings about their unique identity, the value of a supportive friend network becomes even more pronounced. Friends who understand and embrace one's Therian identity can offer tailored advice, empathy, and perspective, smoothing the path in the face of obstacles and ensuring one never feels alone in their journey.

Building Bridges
Beyond personal support, friends often play a crucial role in helping Therians bridge the gap with the larger societal context. By acting as allies, they contribute to broader understanding, acceptance, and integration of Therian identities within diverse social spheres, playing an instrumental role in the continuous endeavor for societal recognition and respect.

In essence, a supportive circle is not just a desirable asset for a Therian but an essential element of their social and emotional ecosystem, contributing fundamentally to their wellbeing, resilience, and growth.

Navigating Friendships Outside the Community

Navigating friendships outside the Therian community poses its own unique set of challenges and rewards. For Therians, these relationships may not have the immediate understanding and shared experiences that bonds within the community do, but they are crucial for a balanced social life and offer their own distinct benefits.

Open Communication
A fundamental aspect of these friendships lies in open and honest communication. For individuals outside the Therian community, understanding this aspect of a friend's identity may take time, patience, and dialogue. Therians can foster these relationships by openly sharing their experiences, feelings, and perspectives, helping their non-Therian friends gain insight into their lives.

Addressing Misunderstandings
Misunderstandings or misconceptions may arise, and addressing them respectfully is essential. Clearing up misconceptions not only strengthens the friendship but also contributes

to broader societal understanding of the Therian community. Offering resources or directing friends to informative platforms can be beneficial in enhancing their understanding.

Mutual Respect
Maintaining friendships with non-Therians also hinges on mutual respect. Both parties should respect each other's beliefs, experiences, and identities, even if they do not fully understand them. This mutual respect lays the foundation for a supportive and enduring friendship.

The Value of Diversity
While shared experiences within the Therian community are invaluable, friendships outside the community offer a diverse perspective on life. These relationships provide opportunities for growth, learning, and mutual enrichment, making them an essential part of a balanced social life.

In conclusion, while navigating friendships outside the Therian community might require additional effort and understanding, the rewards of diverse, enriching relationships and the opportunity to increase awareness and understanding of Therianthropy in society make it an invaluable endeavor.

Online Friendships

In the digital era, online friendships have emerged as significant sources of connection and support, particularly within niche communities like Therians. These virtual bonds can be incredibly enriching, providing emotional sustenance, understanding, and a shared space for discussion and exploration.

The Advantages of Online Friendships
Accessibility: Online platforms break geographical boundaries, enabling Therians worldwide to connect. This global connection is vital for those who may not have local Therian communities, offering them a network of understanding and shared experience.

Anonymity: The digital realm allows Therians to explore and express their identities with a level of anonymity, offering a safe space for those who may not yet be ready to share their identity in their offline lives.

Diverse Perspectives: Online friendships within the Therian community connect individuals with a myriad of experiences, insights, and theriotypes, contributing to a richer, more multifaceted understanding of Therianthropy.

Navigating the Challenges
Physical Presence: While online friendships offer substantial emotional support, the lack of physical presence can be a limitation. Balancing online connections with in-person relationships ensures a well-rounded social network.

Safety: It's paramount to prioritize online safety, ensuring that platforms and connections are secure and respectful.

Strengthening Online Connections
Regular Communication: Consistent and open communication strengthens online friendships, fostering a deep sense of connection and understanding.

Shared Activities: Engaging in online forums, social media groups, or virtual events enhances the bonds between online friends, offering shared experiences even in a virtual format.

Transitioning to Offline: When possible and appropriate, transitioning online friendships to offline connections can add another layer of depth and support to these relationships.

In conclusion, while online friendships within the Therian community may lack physical presence, they hold immense value as sources of support, understanding, and shared experience. Navigating them mindfully ensures they remain a positive and enriching aspect of a Therian's social network.

Family Dynamics

Coming Out as a Therian

Coming out as a Therian is a deeply personal and sometimes emotional process. It involves sharing a fundamental aspect of one's identity with others and can lead to a range of reactions, from warm acceptance to misunderstanding or even hostility.

Preparing for the Conversation
Assess the Situation: It's crucial to gauge the likely reactions of family members. If you anticipate a hostile reaction, it might be worth waiting for a more opportune time or preparing yourself for the possible outcomes.
Gather Information: Having resources and information on hand can help answer questions and alleviate concerns that family members might have. Explain what being a Therian means to you and address misconceptions they might hold.

During the Disclosure
Be Honest but Gentle: Communicate your truth calmly and clearly. Recognize that this may be a lot for them to take in, and give them the time and space to process the information.
Be Prepared for Questions: Family members may have many questions or concerns. Address these patiently, providing clear and concise information to help them understand.

Navigating Negative Reactions
Develop a Support Network: Before coming out, ensure you have a support system in place, whether it's friends, online communities, or mental health professionals who understand your situation.
Maintain Boundaries: If reactions are hostile or unsupportive, establish clear boundaries to protect your emotional well-being.

Moving Forward
Give it Time: Understand that acceptance might not come immediately. Be patient with your family members as they process your disclosure.
Continuous Dialogue: Keep the lines of communication open, offering additional information and addressing concerns as they arise.

In conclusion, coming out as a Therian is a significant step that requires preparation, courage, and resilience. The journey may be challenging, but it can also lead to deeper understanding, acceptance, and a more authentic life.

Balancing Family Expectations

Disclosing a Therian identity may clash with traditional family structures and expectations, presenting a delicate balancing act for many individuals. Traditional and cultural norms can, at times, inadvertently suppress the true essence of a person's identity. It's essential to navigate these challenges with patience, understanding, and clear communication to achieve a semblance of balance and mutual respect.

Understanding Family Concerns
Emphasis on Dialogue: Your family may have preconceived notions or misunderstandings about Therianthropy. Encourage open dialogue, addressing their concerns and providing educational resources to bridge the knowledge gap. Understand that their worries might stem from a place of love and confusion.

Striving for Balance
Compromise: While it's essential to live authentically, sometimes compromise is necessary. Find middle ground where your Therian identity is respected while also acknowledging and respecting your family's values and expectations.
Set Boundaries: Clearly communicate your limits to ensure you are not compromising your well-being for the sake of meeting family expectations. Boundaries are crucial for mutual respect and understanding.

Managing Conflicts
Seek Mediation: If conflicts arise, consider seeking mediation from a trusted family member or professional who understands both perspectives and can facilitate a productive conversation.

Prioritize Your Well-Being: Remember to prioritize your mental and emotional well-being, even if it means making tough decisions about family interactions.

Cultivating Support
Build a Support Network: Establish a robust support network of friends, online communities, and possibly professionals who understand and validate your Therian identity.
Focus on Relationships that Affirm You: Invest time and energy in relationships that affirm your identity and offer emotional support amid family challenges.

In sum, balancing family expectations with a Therian identity is a nuanced journey filled with both challenges and opportunities for growth, understanding, and acceptance. Your well-being and authentic expression should always remain a priority as you navigate these personal and familial waters.

Multi-Generational Therian Families
In some rare but intriguing instances, Therianthropy may appear across generations within a family, offering a unique dynamic and shared understanding that can either strengthen family bonds or add complexity to them.

Navigating the terrain of relationships is a delicate endeavor for anyone, and the Therian identity adds its own set of complexities and enrichments. From the intricacies of romantic entanglements to the unconditional support of true friendship and the often complicated dynamics of family life, being a Therian influences all the relationships you hold dear. Yet, with understanding, open communication, and a dash of courage, these relationships can become a source of endless support and love, helping you fully embrace your unique identity.

Chapter 7: Common Misunderstandings and Criticisms

∞ ∞ ∞

"Amidst the doubts and judgments, stand tall with the strength of your true nature, embracing the truth of your being with unwavering pride."

∞ ∞ ∞

While Therianthropy is gaining gradual acceptance and understanding, it still faces a fair amount of skepticism, misunderstanding, and criticism. Whether these come from mainstream society, scientific communities, or even within the broader alternative spirituality and identity spectrums, it's essential to address them head-on. This chapter aims to clarify some of the common misconceptions, respond to frequent criticisms, and offer strategies for engaging in constructive conversations.

Addressing the Skepticism Around Therianthropy

Scientific Skepticism

Some critics, especially in the scientific community, doubt the validity of Therianthropy due to a lack of empirical evidence. It's important to acknowledge that while personal experiences are valid, they may not fit neatly into established scientific paradigms.

Cultural and Religious Criticism

Therianthropy can sometimes clash with established cultural or religious beliefs, leading to accusations of heresy or deviance. Understanding the cultural context in which such criticisms arise can be crucial for meaningful dialogue.

Internal Community Skepticism

Even within alternative spirituality and identity communities, Therianthropy can face skepticism. The key here is to establish common ground and focus on shared experiences and goals.

Responding to Common Criticisms

"It's Just a Phase"

One frequent criticism is that Therianthropy is a temporary phase or a form of escapism. While the Therian journey can evolve over time, for many, it is a lifelong identity.

"You're Appropriating Indigenous Cultures"

Some argue that the concept of Therianthropy appropriates from indigenous cultures with shape-shifting or animal-spirit beliefs. Respectful dialogue and education about the origins and diversity within Therianthropy can help alleviate these concerns.

"It's a Mental Illness"

Perhaps one of the most damaging criticisms is that Therianthropy is a form of delusion or mental illness. While it's essential to distinguish between identity and pathology, a balanced view acknowledges that Therianthropy usually does not interfere with one's ability to function in daily life.

Strategies for Constructive Conversations

Active Listening

Before you can effectively communicate your viewpoint, it's crucial to understand where the other person is coming from. Listen carefully and ask clarifying questions.

Use Credible Sources

If a debate enters the realm of scientific or academic discussion, citing credible studies or theories can bolster your arguments.

Agree to Disagree

Sometimes, despite your best efforts, you may not reach a mutual understanding. In such cases, it's important to know when to disengage and agree to disagree.

Misunderstandings and criticisms around Therianthropy are as varied as the Therians themselves. Addressing them requires a nuanced approach, blending empathy, education, and sometimes, a thick skin. Through constructive dialogue and a willingness to engage, we can dispel myths, foster understanding, and pave the way for greater acceptance and validation of the diverse tapestry that makes up the Therian community.

Chapter 8: The Therian Code of Ethics

∞ ∞ ∞

"In the respect for life and nature, the therian code flourishes, laying down roots of honor, dignity, and unity."

∞ ∞ ∞

Ethical considerations are integral to the Therian experience. The Therian Code of Ethics is not a universally accepted or prescribed set of rules but rather a compilation of principles and guidelines that many in the community find valuable. These ethics revolve around respect for nature and animals, guidelines for community interaction, and the importance of personal responsibility. In this chapter, we will explore each of these facets in detail.

Respect for Nature and Animals

The Spiritual Connection

For many Therians, the bond with nature and animals is more than just sentimental; it is spiritual. This connection often translates into a commitment to treating nature and its creatures with utmost respect.

Environmental Responsibility

Given the intrinsic connection to the animal kingdom, many Therians feel a strong sense of responsibility towards the environment. This can manifest in various ways, from simple acts like recycling and reducing waste to activism and volunteer work.

Ethical Treatment of Animals

Whether it's pets, wildlife, or animals in agriculture, the ethical treatment of animals is a paramount concern. Many Therians opt for cruelty-free products and advocate for animal rights.

Community Guidelines and Principles

Mutual Respect

The cornerstone of any community is mutual respect. Whether online or at in-person gatherings, treating each other with courtesy is non-negotiable.

Confidentiality and Privacy

Given the sensitive nature of Therian identity, maintaining the confidentiality and privacy of community members is crucial.

Inclusivity and Non-Discrimination

The Therian community is a diverse space. Discrimination based on race, gender, age, or any other characteristic is generally considered unacceptable.

Personal Responsibility

Self-Awareness
As individuals with a unique set of experiences and challenges, Therians are encouraged to engage in constant self-reflection to better understand their identity and how it interacts with the world around them.

Accountability
Being a Therian does not exempt one from societal rules or personal accountability. If your actions cause harm, whether to others or to the environment, taking responsibility is essential.

Balance and Harmony
Living as a Therian means balancing your human life with your Therian identity. Striving for harmony between the two not only enriches your life but also stands as a testament to the responsible integration of this unique identity.

Ethics in the Therian community, while not monolithic, revolve around core principles that emphasize respect, responsibility, and community well-being. By adhering to these principles, Therians not only enrich their own lives but also contribute positively to the broader community and the world at large. These ethical considerations form the foundation upon which a fulfilling and responsible Therian life can be built.

Chapter 9: The Practice of Quadrobics

∞ ∞ ∞

"In the rhythmic dance of quadrobics, embrace the primal pulse of the earth, uniting body and spirit in the ancient cadence of four-footed harmony."

∞ ∞ ∞

Quadrobics, the practice of moving on all fours, is more than a physical exercise for many in the Therian community. For some, it serves as a form of spiritual meditation, a way to connect more deeply with their theriotype. For others, it can be an exploratory practice to understand the physicality of the animal with which they identify. In this chapter, we will delve into what quadrobics is, its importance within the Therian community, and how you can safely practice it.

The Origin of Quadrobics

From Physical Training to Spiritual Practice

While quadrobics initially gained traction as a form of physical exercise, it has evolved within the Therian community into a more holistic practice encompassing physical, psychological, and sometimes spiritual dimensions.

Psychological and Spiritual Benefits

Mind-Body Connection

Quadrobics can strengthen the mind-body connection, enhancing both self-awareness and body awareness.

Spiritual Resonance

For some, the act of moving on all fours brings them closer to their theriotype, creating a sense of spiritual resonance.

Guidelines for Practicing Quadrobics Safely

Physical Precautions

Given that the human body isn't naturally designed for sustained movement on all fours, certain precautions should be taken to avoid injury.

Setting Boundaries

It's crucial to know your limits and to practice in a safe and supportive environment.

Whether you engage in quadrobics for the physical benefits, psychological insights, or spiritual connections, this unique practice offers an additional avenue for Therians to explore their identities. As with any form of practice, it is crucial to approach it with an open mind, proper preparation, and a respect for your own limits and boundaries.

Chapter 10: Modern Perspectives: A Journey Through the Digital Age and Beyond

∞ ∞ ∞

"In the pulsing veins of the digital realm, let the Therian spirit roam free, transcending pixels and wires to weave the tapestry of collective identity, understanding, and unity in the boundless world beyond."

∞ ∞ ∞

As society progresses and technology evolves, so does our understanding of identity and spirituality. In a world where information is at our fingertips and communities can be formed in the blink of an eye, modern Therianthropy has taken on new dimensions that differ from its historical roots. While the essence of identifying as a non-human animal on an integral level remains the same, the ways in which Therians connect, learn, and express themselves have been revolutionized.

Online Communities

The rise of online forums, social media, and platforms like TikTok has provided a unique space for Therians to connect, share experiences, and even 'howl' in the digital world.

TikTok, with its visual medium and short video format, offers a unique platform for Therians to showcase their shifts, tales, and personal journeys. While TikTok offers vast reach, it also poses challenges such as skepticism, trolling, and misrepresentation. How do Therians navigate these waters?

Beyond TikTok, what lies on the horizon for digital Therian communities? A speculative glance at the potential of virtual reality, augmented reality, and more.

Virtual Reality

Virtual spaces offer an unprecedented realm for Therians to explore their identities. From VR chatrooms to fully immersive environments, Therians can experience their theriotypes in ways previously unimaginable. The potential for VR to host Therian gatherings where individuals can meet, connect, and share experiences beyond the constraints of geography.

While VR holds the promise of unparalleled exploration, expression, and connection, it also necessitates thoughtful engagement to ensure it serves the wellbeing and advancement of the Therian community.

Mainstream Recognition

While Therianthropy is still often misunderstood, there has been growing interest in the psychological community to study and understand it, providing a layer of validation and reducing stigma.

Self-Acceptance

Modern psychology promotes the importance of self-acceptance and mental well-being, aspects that are integral to the Therian journey.

Skepticism and Misunderstanding

In our ever-evolving world, where identity and personal expression are celebrated more than ever, Therianthropy remains a realm that is met with raised brows and hushed whispers. Often relegated to the outskirts of mainstream understanding, the concept of Therianthropy is enshrouded in skepticism and misunderstanding. Yet, for those who identify as Therians, this is a journey of the soul—a profound alignment with an inner animalistic self.

Modern Therianthropy isn't just a relic of ancient beliefs or a passing phase; it's a nuanced identity that is intertwined with today's digital age, the realms of psychology, and the ever-pertinent discussions on ethics. While ancient civilizations might have had shamanistic practices that resonated with therianthropic ideas, today's Therians often find community and understanding in online forums, YouTube channels, and social media platforms. This digital embracement allows for a vast network of interconnected individuals who, despite geographical distances, share a common thread of experience and self-recognition.

Yet, as with any identity or belief that challenges conventional norms, Therianthropy is often met with skepticism. Detractors may dismiss it as mere escapism, a delusion, or a bid for attention. Some argue from a scientific standpoint, seeking empirical evidence of such an identity, while others may resort to cultural or religious arguments to counteract the claims of Therians.

The psychological intersection is particularly poignant. While some critics hastily label Therianthropy as a form of dissociation or a psychological 'condition', many Therians find solace in understanding that their identity, though different, is an intrinsic part of their psyche. It's not a maladjustment or disorder but a deep-seated resonance with an inner nature.

Ethical considerations further complicate the narrative. As Therians advocate for understanding and acceptance, they must navigate a world where the line between appropriation and genuine identity is continually scrutinized. Ethical Therianthropy respects cultural contexts, ensuring that one's therianthropic identity doesn't inadvertently appropriate or belittle the beliefs and practices of indigenous or other communities.

Despite the challenges, the Therian journey, at its core, is a quest for authenticity—a pursuit of understanding and aligning with one's truest self. It's a testament to the human spirit's resilience and its eternal yearning for self-realization. As the world continues to evolve, so too does the narrative around Therianthropy, ever-shifting, ever-resilient, and ever-persistent in its quest for acceptance and understanding.

Chapter 11: Embracing Your Inner Nature

∞ ∞ ∞

"Let the embrace of your inner nature be the loving arms that hold you, as you traverse the paths of self-discovery and acceptance."

∞ ∞ ∞

The journey to fully embracing your Therian identity is deeply personal and continually evolving. At its core, this process involves significant self-acceptance, creative expression, and the nurturing of your unique traits and abilities. In this concluding chapter, we will explore the importance of accepting your inner nature, provide tips for embodying your Therian identity more fully, and examine the vital role of creativity and imagination in this journey.

The Importance of Self-Acceptance

Inner Harmony

Self-acceptance is the first step towards achieving inner harmony. Accepting your Therian identity as an intrinsic part of who you are can be liberating and provide a sense of inner peace.

Overcoming Social and Cultural Barriers

The journey to self-acceptance often involves overcoming societal stereotypes and cultural taboos. By embracing your Therian identity, you empower yourself to live authentically, irrespective of external judgments.

The Link to Mental Well-being

Studies and personal testimonies within the community often indicate that self-acceptance plays a crucial role in overall mental well-being, making it a critical aspect of embracing your Therian nature.

Tips for Embracing Your Therian Identity

Journaling

Capturing your thoughts, feelings, and experiences related to your Therian identity can provide both clarity and validation.

Therian Rituals

Whether it's a howl at the moon or a quiet moment in nature, incorporating Therian rituals into your daily life can offer a grounding experience.

Join a Community

Whether online or offline, becoming part of a Therian community can offer invaluable support and guidance.

The Role of Creativity and Imagination

Expressive Arts

Painting, writing, music, or any other form of artistic expression can be a powerful way to explore and celebrate your Therian identity.

Creative Visualization

Imagination is a tool that can help you connect more deeply with your theriotype. Visualization exercises can offer both insight and emotional connection.

Play and Exploration

Never underestimate the power of play. Engaging in activities that allow you to express your Therian traits can be both fun and enlightening.

Embracing your inner nature is a lifelong journey, filled with its own sets of challenges and rewards. Self-acceptance is the cornerstone of this journey, serving as the basis for a fulfilling life that honors your unique identity. Creativity and imagination not only make this journey more enjoyable but also offer avenues for deeper understanding and expression. As we close this book, remember that the journey of a thousand miles begins with a single step—or paw print. Here's to you, and here's to embracing your unique and wondrous inner nature.

Chapter 12: Your Personal Therian Experience: A Space for Reflection

∞ ∞ ∞

"In the sacred pages of personal reflection, let your therian journey unfold, painting the landscape of your soul with the hues of experience, insight, and transformation."

∞ ∞ ∞

As you navigate the winding path of Therianthropy, you'll find that your experiences are as unique as you are. This section is a blank canvas for you to capture those moments, thoughts, or feelings that define your Therian journey. Whether it's a memorable dream, a spiritual connection you felt, or simply day-to-day experiences that make you who you are, this space is for you.

Prompts to Consider:

If you're unsure where to begin, here are some prompts that might help you get started:
- Describe the moment you realized you identify as a Therian.
- What emotions or sensations do you experience during shifts?
- Have you ever felt misunderstood because of your Therian identity? How did you handle it?
- Write about an experience where you felt a strong connection to your theriotype.
- How has being a Therian influenced your perspective on life, relationships, or spirituality?

A page for personal reflection

Feel free to write, sketch, or even paste pictures that resonate with your experience. There's no right or wrong way to use this space—it's entirely yours to fill.

....
....
....
....
....
....
....
....
....
....

Bonus Quiz: How Therian Are You?

This quiz is a simple tool to encourage reflection and exploration about your connection with therianthropy. Your identity and experiences are personal and unique. This quiz is not definitive but a step towards understanding your feelings and thoughts.

Q1: Do you feel a profound emotional and spiritual connection with a certain animal?
Always
Sometimes
Never

Q2: Do you experience shifts where you feel more like an animal than a human?
Always
Sometimes
Never

Q3: Do you believe that you have an animal soul or spirit?
Always
Sometimes
Never

Q4: Do you feel more at home in nature or in the presence of the animal you identify with?
Always
Sometimes
Never

Q5: Have you researched therianthropy and related spiritual beliefs?
Always
Sometimes
Never

Q6: Do you participate in online or offline therian communities?
Always
Sometimes
Never

Q7: Do you have dreams or visions where you embody an animal form?
Always
Sometimes
Never

Q8: Do you feel uncomfortable or out of place in your human body?
Always
Sometimes

Never

Results:

Mostly Always:
You strongly identify with therian experiences. Your connection with a specific animal or animals is a significant part of your identity. Continue exploring this aspect of yourself and engaging with supportive communities.

Mostly Sometimes:
You might have some therianthropic feelings or experiences. Take your time to explore these feelings further and seek out more information and support.

Mostly Never:
You may not identify closely with therian experiences, and that's completely okay. Everyone has a unique path and identity.

Note:
Regardless of the results, it's essential to understand that your feelings and identity are valid. This quiz is a guide and should not dictate or define your identity. It's always beneficial to continue exploring your identity and feelings, seeking support, and learning more about yourself and the world around you

Conclusion

∞ ∞ ∞

"As the pages close, let the journey echo, a melody of self, spirit, and the embracing arms of the wild within. May the paths ahead bloom, bathed in the light of understanding, acceptance, and unyielding Therian pride."

∞ ∞ ∞

Summary of Key Takeaways

As we reach the end of "Therian Tales: Embracing Our Inner Nature," it's important to reflect on the journey we've embarked upon together through these pages.

- Understanding the Basics: The first step in any journey is understanding what you're embarking upon. We explored the historical context, definitions, and diverse experiences that make up the Therian community.
- Psychological and Spiritual Dimensions: The Therian experience is multifaceted, with psychological theories providing one lens and spiritual beliefs offering another. Both are integral in understanding the complex nature of Therianthropy.
- Community and Relationships: No person is an island, and the support network around you plays a vital role in your Therian journey. Whether it's romantic relationships, friendships, or family dynamics, your interactions with others have a significant impact on your experience.
- Ethical Considerations: The Therian Code of Ethics, though not universally standardized, offers important guidelines for interaction within the community and provides a blueprint for responsible living.
- Embracing Your Identity: The final leg of this journey involves internalization. Self-acceptance and the incorporation of Therian traits into your daily life are essential for a balanced and fulfilling experience.

Encouragement to Continue the Journey of Self-Discovery and Acceptance

This book serves merely as a primer, a first step in your exploration of what it means to be a Therian. The road ahead is one that only you can walk, filled with its unique challenges and triumphs. There will be times of doubt, where you may question your identity or face skepticism from others. However, these moments are just as much a part of the journey as the times of affirmation and joy.

Never underestimate the power of community and never hesitate to seek guidance and friendship from those who walk a similar path. Yet, also know that your Therian identity is your own—unique in its expression and meaningful in its intricacy.

Self-discovery is a never-ending process, and self-acceptance is a goal that continually moves with you as you grow and evolve. Keep exploring, keep questioning, and keep embracing the wondrous being that you are.

Thank you for sharing this part of your journey with us. May your path be filled with enlightenment, your steps guided by integrity, and your heart lifted by the joy of embracing your true inner nature.

Here's to you, and to the endless journey of self-discovery and acceptance that lies ahead.

Appendix

Frequently Asked Questions

What is Therianthropy?

Therianthropy refers to the identification, either spiritual or psychological, with an animal species other than human. This can manifest in a range of experiences, from dreams and spiritual beliefs to specific behaviors and preferences.

Is Therianthropy a Religion?

No, Therianthropy is not a religion, although some Therians incorporate spiritual beliefs into their identity. It is more accurately described as a subculture or identity that can exist independently of religious beliefs.

How Do I Know If I'm a Therian?

The journey to identifying as a Therian is deeply personal and varies from individual to individual. It often involves significant self-reflection, exploration, and sometimes, interaction with a supportive community.

Can You Be More Than One Theriotype?

Yes, some individuals identify with multiple theriotypes. This is known as being a polytherian.

Resource List: Books, Articles, Websites, and Communities

Books

- "The Field Guide to Otherkin" by Lupa
- "Animal-Speak" by Ted Andrews

Websites

- Therian wiki: A comprehensive platform for Therians offering forums, articles, and community resources. (therian.fantom.com)

Youtube channels

- "Wikihow"
- "Therianterritory"
- "phenicfox"

Communities
- Therian guide community: (https://forums.therian-guide.com/portal.php)
- Various subreddits like r/Therian and r/Otherkin
- Amino Therian Community: A mobile community for Therians

Acknowledgments

Putting together a book like "Therian Tales: Embracing Our Inner Nature" has been a collaborative endeavour in the truest sense. I would like to express my deepest gratitude to all who have contributed their time, knowledge, and support to make this project a reality.

Firstly, I extend my heartfelt thanks to the numerous Therians who courageously shared their personal stories, insights, and experiences. Your openness has been invaluable, adding depth and authenticity to the narrative.

I would also like to thank the scholars, psychologists, and spiritual leaders who agreed to be interviewed for this book. Your expertise lent a level of rigor and credibility that greatly enriched the content.

A special thanks goes out to the online communities—forums, subreddits, and social media groups—where countless individuals offered support, advice, and constructive criticism during the research phase. Your collective wisdom was a guiding light.

I'm incredibly grateful to my editorial team for their meticulous attention to detail, and for their unwavering patience and encouragement throughout the writing process.

I would also like to thank my friends and family for their unwavering support and understanding, especially during those long nights and tight deadlines. Your belief in the importance of this work was a constant source of motivation.

Last but certainly not least, I wish to express my gratitude to you, the reader. Thank you for embarking on this journey with me. Your curiosity, engagement, and willingness to explore the complexities of Therian identity make all the effort worthwhile.

May this book serve as a starting point for many on their journey toward understanding and embracing their unique inner nature. Thank you, one and all, for making this project not only possible but deeply meaningful.

Author,
Uranzaya Batsaikhan

Printed in Great Britain
by Amazon